Fact Finders®

ADVENTURES ON THE AMERICAN FRONTIER

SURVIVING THE JOURNEY

THE STORY OF THE OREGON TRAIL

BY DANNY KRAVITZ

Consultant:
Michael J. Trinklein
Professor Emeritus
Idaho State University
Pocatello, Idaho

CAPSTONE PRESS
a capstone imprint

Fact Finders Books are published by Capstone Press,
1710 Roe Crest Drive, North Mankato, Minnesota 56003
www.capstonepub.com

LIBRARY OF CONGRESS CATALOGING-IN-PUBLICATION DATA

Kravitz, Danny, 1970–

Surviving the journey : the story of the Oregon Trail / by Danny Kravitz.

pages cm.—(Fact finders: adventures on the American frontier)

Includes bibliographical references and index.

Summary: "Examines the Oregon Trail by discussing how and why it came to be and the immediate and lasting effects it had on the nation and the people who traveled it"—Provided by publisher.

ISBN 978-1-4914-0187-3 (library binding)

ISBN 978-1-4914-0192-7 (paperback)

ISBN 978-1-4914-0196-5 (ebook PDF)

1. Oregon National Historic Trail—Juvenile literature. 2. Frontier and pioneer life—West (U.S.)—Juvenile literature. 3. Overland journeys to the Pacific—Juvenile literature. 4. West (U.S.)—History—19th century—Juvenile literature. 5. Oregon Territory—History—Juvenile literature. I. Title.

F597.K73 2014

978'.02—dc23   2014013066

EDITORIAL CREDITS

Jennifer Huston, editor; Sarah Bennett, series designer; Kazuko Collins, layout artist; Wanda Winch, media researcher; Tori Abraham, production specialist

PHOTO CREDITS

Capstone, 7, 22; Courtesy of the Federal Highway Administration, artist Carl Rakeman, 27; Courtesy of L. Tom Perry Special Collections, Brigham Young University, 23; Courtesy of Scotts Bluff National Monument: William Henry Jackson, 14, 15, 17, 20; CRIAimages: Jay Robert Nash Collection, 12 (right); Getty Images Inc: American Stock, 10, Blank Archives, 19, Fotosearch, 12 (left); Jim Carson, jimcarsonstudio.com, cover, 6, 25; Library of Congress: Prints and Photographs Division, 21; North Wind Picture Archives, 9, 28; Oregon Trail Family, 1848 ©Morgan Weistling, licensed by The Greenwich Workshop, Inc. www.greenwichworkshop.com, 5; Shutterstock: 06photo, book page bkgrnd, homey design, leather design, Itana, sunburst design, ixer, 1 (banner), LongQuattro, 7, 22 (compass), Picsfive, parchment paper design, Zack Frank, 11; Tales of the Day ©Heide Presse, 13; Whitman College Manuscript Collection, Whitman College and Northwest Collections, 18

PRIMARY SOURCE BIBLIOGRAPHY

Page 17—Wyeth, John B. *Oregon, a Short History of a Long Journey ...*, 1833.

Page 18—Schlissel, Lillian. *Women's Diaries of the Westward Journey*. New York: Schocken Books, 2004.

Page 24—Lenox, Edward Henry. *Overland to Oregon in the Tracks of Lewis and Clarke*. Oakland, Calif.: Dowdle Press, 1993.

Printed in the United States of America in Stevens Point, Wisconsin.

032014   008092WZF14

TABLE OF CONTENTS

— ◆ —

CHAPTER 1

THE ADVENTURE OF A LIFETIME

A young boy lies on the ground looking up at the bright twinkling stars that reach across the sky like a river. He hears something rustling in the grass. Maybe it's a snake! Or maybe it's just the wind moving the dusty earth.

Back at camp, the women have just finished cleaning up after dinner. The men sit around the campfire. Some are playing music as children dance nearby. Others tend to their animals and check their supplies.

The boy looks at the huge rock formation in front of him. They call it Independence Rock. Everyone on this journey has written their names on it. It is a symbol of their freedom to explore the frontier and move out West.

The boy and his family are traveling west on the Oregon Trail. Journeying across America in covered wagons, they and hundreds of others are making the long trek across the country. They are on the adventure of a lifetime!

The Lewis and Clark expedition paved the way for pioneers who wanted to explore the West.

The Quest to Go West

The Oregon Trail is the path American settlers used to travel to the western United States in the mid-1800s. In 1804, President Thomas Jefferson sent Meriwether Lewis and William Clark to find a route to the Pacific Ocean. Lewis and Clark made it to the Pacific, but their route was not fit for wagons. Over time, fur traders and mountain men carved a westward path across the plains and through the rugged Rockies. This route eventually came to be called the Oregon Trail.

Route of the Oregon Trail

Within a few decades, thousands of American settlers were moving west. Some went for adventure on the frontier and a new life out West. Some were eager to discover gold. Still others sought religious freedom. But many made the difficult journey because they dreamed of a better life for themselves and their families. In the West, they hoped to find fertile land and good weather for farming.

The Great Migration

In 1843 the Oregon Country's **provisional government** gave 640 acres (259 hectares) of land to male citizens who moved there. This inspired about 1,000 people to move out West. That first wagon train was known as the Great Migration. During the next 25 years, more than half a million people traveled the Oregon Trail.

MORMON TRAIL

In the mid-1800s, more than 70,000 Mormons **migrated** to Salt Lake City, Utah, to start their own religious community. They traveled west along the Mormon Trail, which paralleled the Oregon Trail on the north side of the Platte River. After the Platte split into two branches, the two trails followed the same path for the next 550 miles (885 kilometers). At Fort Bridger in Wyoming, the Mormons headed southwest to Salt Lake City.

provisional government—a temporary government; the provisional government of the Oregon Country served as a temporary form of government until Oregon became a state
migrate—to move from one place to another

7

CHAPTER 2

WESTWARD HO!
THE JOURNEY BEGINS

For many pioneers, the 2,000-mile (3,219-km) Oregon Trail began in Independence, Missouri. But some folks had to travel for hundreds of miles just to get there.

In Independence, excitement filled the air. Thousands of settlers prepared for the journey. Children made new friends with other children who were going west. Parents did the same because forming wagon trains helped people herd and guard their animals. It also ensured that travelers had help from one another along the way.

Settlers usually set out in springtime, which meant that the days were getting warmer and the prairie grass was growing high. The settlers were thankful for the tall grass of the prairies because it kept their livestock fed.

What to Bring?

Typically families brought a wagon or two. Oxen pulled the wagons better than mules, which could be stubborn and unruly. Oxen were big and slow, but they were steady and reliable.

Families also took cows for milk, as well as horses, food, utensils, clothing, and camping gear. Men brought along guns and knives for hunting and protection. The pioneers also carried shovels, axes, plows, and other tools in the wagons because they would need them for farming once they reached Oregon.

Some people tried to bring furniture or stoves, but these items were simply too heavy to transport. Many folks were only a few miles into their journey when they realized they had over-packed their wagons. With no other choice, they began throwing things out.

THE DANGERS OF GETTING A LATE START

Snowstorms come early in the mountains. If settlers left too late in the spring, they risked getting trapped in the mountains near the end of the trail. That could be deadly! They also had a better chance of finding clean water the earlier they left. That is, water that wasn't contaminated with diseases like **cholera**.

cholera—a dangerous disease that causes severe sickness and diarrhea; cholera is caused by contaminated food or water

Life on the Trail

On the Oregon Trail, settlers typically woke before sunrise and had hot coffee, biscuits, and bacon for breakfast. Then they'd start moving along with the wagon train. They were never quite sure what challenges the day might bring. Bad weather, hunger, difficult water crossings, and broken wagon wheels were all part of the experience. At midday folks stopped to rest and eat dry bread and bacon for lunch. There were a lot of meals of bread and bacon on the Oregon Trail.

People usually walked instead of riding in the wagon. Walking meant less weight in the wagons and less strain on the animals pulling them. Added weight could also damage the wheels or cause the wagons to get stuck in the mud.

The trail was often very dry and dusty. With so many people, animals, and wagons kicking up dirt, thick clouds of dust formed in the air. Things got pretty dirty—especially for those at the back of the pack. For that reason, the wagons fanned out across wide, open prairies. When the trail narrowed, the settlers took turns at the back of the wagon train.

THE PRAIRIE SCHOONER

A prairie schooner was a covered wagon popular with pioneers and settlers in the 1800s. It had a white canvas cover or "bonnet" with drawstrings to open and close the front and back. From a distance the covered wagon looked like a small sailing ship or "schooner." And because it crossed the prairies, it soon had its nickname—the prairie schooner.

For the long journey west, a family of four would need to pack the following:

Bacon—400–700 pounds (181–318 kilograms)

Beans—200 pounds (91 kg)

Coffee—75 pounds (34 kg)

Flour—600–800 pounds (272–363 kg)

Rice—a sack or two

Sugar—100 pounds (45 kg)

Tea—4 pounds (1.8 kg)

Canvas bonnet top that could be closed in the back and front during bad weather.

Wagon box for carrying supplies.

Barrel used to store water for cooking and drinking.

All the supplies and possessions a family could pack were carried in the wagon.

The hitch attached the wagon to oxen or mules.

Iron-rimmed wheels were smaller in the front for making sharp turns.

BUFFALO CHIPS

In some areas. there weren't a lot of trees for firewood, so settlers burned buffalo **dung** for cooking and to keep warm. It was a bit messy, but it burned well. And surprisingly, it gave off only a slight odor. Imagine what a funny sight it was to see people searching for the biggest, driest pieces of buffalo dung! Children even made a game of it, tossing these buffalo "chips" back and forth.

Setting Up Camp

By the time the wagon train stopped for the night, everyone was exhausted. Fifteen miles (24 km) of walking outside will do that to anyone, even on nice days. At night, the men parked the wagons in a large circle. The animals were kept inside the circle to prevent them from wandering off. Then the men tended to the livestock while children gathered fuel for fires and the women made dinner. Dinner was usually more bacon, beans, and bread. Sometimes the settlers ate fish, antelope, buffalo, or other food they had hunted.

dung—solid waste from animals

After dinner the adults gathered around the campfire and talked or told stories. The children danced or played games. But sleep came quickly. Some folks slept in tents, although many bunked on the ground under a blanket of stars. The men took turns keeping watch for animals or American Indians. Waking up stiff and sore in the morning was all part of the experience.

CHAPTER 3

THE FRONTIER AWAITS

Traveling through Kansas, the pioneers crossed grassy flatlands and rolling hills. Some of the many creeks along the way had steep banks that required settlers to dig a path for the wagons. Some rivers had to be crossed by ferry. There was even a toll bridge across the Kansas River near Topeka. It cost a dollar to cross.

Travelers on the Oregon Trail often stopped at Alcove Spring in Kansas for a brief rest and fresh drinking water.

14

About a week after crossing the Kansas River, settlers arrived at a campsite called Alcove Spring. There, crystal clear, cold water tumbled down a 12-foot- (3.7-meter-) high rock formation into a basin surrounded by thriving shrubs. The comfort and charm of Alcove Spring made it tempting to stay, but the goal was to get to Oregon. So onward the wagons rolled.

Fort Kearny

After traveling about 150 miles (241 km) across the grassy plains of Nebraska, the settlers arrived at Fort Kearny. This outpost in the south-central part of the state was built to protect those traveling the Oregon Trail. There they could buy supplies, get medical help, have their wagons repaired, and even send mail.

FRIEND OR FOE?

At first, many pioneers were afraid of the American Indians. But most of the Indians they encountered were helpful and friendly. They traded buffalo skins and moccasins with the settlers. They helped them find animals that had strayed away from the wagon train. They also helped the pioneers push wagons out of the mud when they got stuck. Many times American Indians saved settlers from drowning during dangerous river crossings.

ᝪᝪ FUN FACT ᝪᝪ

A man named David McCanles owned a bridge at Rock Creek Station in Nebraska. He charged people to cross it, but the price depended on how much it looked like they could afford! He charged anywhere from 10 cents to $1.50.

WHERE THE BUFFALO ROAMED

American buffalo, or bison, are massive animals that can weigh up to 2,000 pounds (907 kg). Thousands of buffalo once stampeded across the plains, kicking up dust for miles. These enormous herds sometimes blocked the wagon trains for hours.

Many men took to hunting the buffalo. American Indians also hunted buffalo, but they used nearly every portion of the animals for food and clothing. Many white settlers killed the animals simply for the fun of it, which greatly reduced the buffalo population. At the start of the 1800s, there were more than 20 million American buffalo. By the 1890s they were nearly extinct, with less than 1,000 remaining.

The Muddy Platte River

After leaving Fort Kearny, it was time to follow the Platte River … for the next 450 miles (724 km)! The Platte River was shallow but muddy with a swampy bottom. As settlers followed the river west, the prairie grass became shorter, and fewer trees lined the trail. Luckily, they still had plenty of buffalo chips to keep their campfires burning!

Crossing the Platte

About a week after the settlers left Fort Kearny, the Platte River split into two branches. They needed to follow the north branch of the river into Wyoming. But to do so, they first had to cross the South Platte River. Old California Crossing was a good place to cross the Platte River because the water was only a few feet deep. But it was also more than a mile wide, and river crossings were dangerous. People and animals could drown, float away, or get crushed by wagons tipping over.

White men hunted buffalo for sport and to get them out of the way of the wagon trains.

Not long after crossing the Platte River, the pioneers faced a downward slope called Windlass Hill. The hill was so steep that the wagons could roll too fast and crash. The pioneers attached ropes and pulled backward to slow down the wagons. If they lost control, the wagons would crash to the bottom.

"We saw them in frightful droves, as far as the eye could reach, appearing at a distance as if the ground itself was moving like the sea ... [They] have no fear of man. They will travel over him, and make nothing of him."

—Pioneer John B. Wyeth describing the enormous herds of buffalo, 1832

Narcissa Whitman

PIONEERING WOMEN ON THE TRAIL

Narcissa Whitman and Eliza Spalding were the first white women to travel the Oregon Trail and cross the **Continental Divide**.

In 1836 Whitman helped her husband, Marcus, build and operate a mission in southeastern Washington. Eliza Spalding and her husband, Henry, became the first white settlers in Idaho. It was a rigorous and rugged life that they had chosen. As Narcissa Whitman stated at the time, it was "an unheard of journey for females."

Once they got down the hill, they arrived at Ash Hollow, which was dotted with refreshing shade trees and beautiful wildflowers. And the crisp, clean water was the best the settlers had tasted since they first started their journey. Many travelers rested there for a few days.

Hardships and Sacrifices

For all its beauty, the Oregon Trail could be brutal. Every day brought hard work, the threat of danger, and the chance for disaster. Many settlers died on the trail long before ever reaching Oregon. People drowned. Accidental gunshots caused injuries and deaths. Being run over by a wagon wheel or stampeding livestock was common and could be deadly.

"Rained all night; is still raining. I have just counted 17 wagons traveling ahead of us in the mud and water. No feed for our poor stock to be got at any price. Have to feed them flour and meal. Traveled 22 miles [35 km] today."

—Amelia Stewart Knight, April 21, 1853

But the greatest killer was disease, and cholera was the worst. Cholera caused digestive problems and dehydration that most often led to death. Some victims woke up fine in the morning, were infected with the disease by afternoon, and were dead by nightfall. Others lingered and suffered as they bounced along in their wagons.

The dead were buried right along the trail. There were an average of 10 graves per mile on the Oregon Trail.

Life was hard on the Oregon Trail. Many people did not survive the journey.

Continental Divide—an invisible line that splits North America into two parts

4

THE JOURNEY CONTINUES

Before leaving Nebraska and entering Wyoming, settlers encountered several wondrous rock formations. To the pioneers, Courthouse Rock and its neighbor Jail Rock, looked like giant castles made of sandstone and clay. They each stood over 400 feet (122 m) high.

With its 300-foot (91-m) spire, Chimney Rock was visible from 30 miles (48 km) away. The highest point of Scotts Bluff reached more than 800 feet (244 m) into the sky.

After a few more weeks of rough wilderness, the settlers reached Fort Laramie in Wyoming. The weary travelers welcomed the chance to rest and buy supplies at this outpost.

Independence Rock

About 200 miles (322 km) west of Fort Laramie, Independence Rock symbolized America's freedom. Settlers carved their names on it to show they were there. Many of the names can still be seen today.

Devil's Gate

A few miles further southwest, settlers came upon Devil's Gate—a narrow **gorge** through a large rock formation. It was so narrow that wagons had to go around it. So many deaths happened at Devil's Gate that some people thought it was cursed. But that didn't stop people from trying to climb it.

Devil's Gate

DON'T BLAME THE COW!

In 1854, near Fort Laramie, a cow wandered away from a wagon train and into a Sioux village. The Sioux killed the animal for food. The soldiers at Fort Laramie, who were there to protect the settlers, confronted the American Indians. Realizing their mistake, the Indians offered to give the soldiers a horse in return. But Lieutenant Grattan ordered his soldiers to shoot at the tribe. The Sioux chief told his warriors not to fight back. Grattan ordered his soldiers to fire again. This time they killed the chief. After that the warriors fought back, and Grattan and nearly all of his men were killed.

gorge—a canyon with steep walls that rise straight upward

21

MTS.

ROCKY

Columbia

Oregon City
OREGON COUNTRY

Fort Boise

CASCADE

Snake

Fort Hall

Independence Rock

N. Platte

Umbolsr

Great
Salt Lake

Fort
Bridger

MTS.

Fort
Laramie

Chimney Rock

LOUISIANA

Missouri

Red

Missouri

Mississippi

Great Lakes

Fort Kearny

Kansas

Independence

Ohio

Atlantic
Ocean

Colorado

Santa Fe

Arkansas

PURCHASE

Mississippi

Pacific
Ocean

Rio Grande

Gulf of Mexico

Louisiana Purchase	☐	Fort
← Oregon Trail		
← California Trail		
◄···· Hastings Cutoff		

South Pass

With the hot sun beating down on the dusty trail, the settlers reached South Pass in southwestern Wyoming. This gateway to the West marked the halfway point on their journey.

About 130 miles (209 km) southwest of South Pass, the pioneers came to Fort Bridger. This spot was about 1,200 miles (1,931 km) along the trail. But those headed to Oregon still had 800 miles (1,287 km) left to go! At Fort Bridger, the Mormon Trail branched off toward Salt Lake City, about 100 miles (161 km) further south and west. Those heading to Oregon and California continued northwest to Fort Hall in southern Idaho. About 50 miles (80 km) after Fort Hall, the California Trail veered off to the southwest toward Nevada.

Crossing the Snake River ... or Not

A few days after leaving Fort Hall, the pioneers had to decide whether or not to cross the Snake River. They could cross at a place called Three Island Crossing, but it was extremely dangerous. The other option was to stay on the south side of the river. But this was a much longer route.

"We lost two of our men, Ayres and Stringer ... Ayres ... got into trouble with his mules in crossing the stream. Stringer ... went to his relief, and both of them were drowned in sight of their women folks ... The bodies were never recovered."

—Edward Henry Lenox recalling a deadly Snake River crossing in 1843

Fort Boise

Those who crossed the Snake River ended up at Fort Boise. When the pioneers arrived there, they were still about 350 miles (563 km) from their destination—the Willamette Valley. Some weary settlers wanted to rest at Fort Boise for a few days, but they had to keep going. If they didn't, they risked getting caught in bad weather. It was mid-September and they worried about getting caught in early snowstorms. They also worried about getting stranded in the mountains like the Donner Party.

The Donner Party

In 1846 Jacob and George Donner led a group of nearly 90 pioneers headed to California. The Donners had heard about a quicker route across Utah and Nevada, so they decided to try it. But the shortcut had never been attempted with wagons, and trying it cost them dearly. It slowed them down, and they lost several horses, cows, and wagons. By late October heavy snowfall had trapped them in the Sierra Nevada Mountains, near the border of California and Nevada. Bitterly cold temperatures and starvation soon left many dead. Surviving members were forced to eat the flesh of some of the deceased to keep from starving to death. Only about half of the original group made it out alive.

CHAPTER 5

ARE WE THERE YET?

When the pioneers reached an area called The Dalles in present-day north-central Oregon, the trail came to an abrupt end. The Cascade Mountains were blocking the way. But the settlers' final destination was still almost 100 miles (161 km) further west.

In order to get past the Cascades, the settlers had to float their wagons down the Columbia River on rafts. With its bumpy rapids, dangerous currents, and swirling whirlpools, the river was impassable in spots. Also strong wind gusts could flip over the rafts. Settlers often hired American Indians to help them navigate this violent stretch. In some places, such as Cascade Falls, the settlers had no choice but to **portage** their belongings around the falls.

portage—to carry a boat or supplies over land from one stretch of water to another

In order to get around the Cascade Mountains, some settlers chose to ferry their wagons down the Columbia River.

Some folks avoided the river altogether. In the mid-1840s a path known as the Barlow Road was cut through the forests of Mount Hood. But this route wasn't any easier. The slopes were so steep that wagons and oxen often slid right off the trail. And snowstorms were always a danger for those who attempted this route.

After a long, hard journey on the Oregon Trail, the settlers were finally able to settle down and build homes.

TIMELINE

1804
Explorers Lewis and Clark set off on a journey to the Pacific Ocean.

1840
Joel Walker is the first settler to travel the Oregon Trail with children.

1843
Approximately 1,000 people travel to Oregon as part of the Great Migration.

1804

1840

1842

1844

1836
Narcissa Whitman and Eliza Spalding become the first white women to travel the Oregon Trail and cross the Continental Divide.

We Have Arrived

Whichever route they took through the Cascades, the settlers arrived at the same place—the Willamette Valley in present-day northwestern Oregon. After traveling 2,000 miles (3,219 km) through snow, rain, and blistering heat, the pioneers had reached their destination. They'd encountered American Indians, seen wild animals, faced hunger and death, and witnessed amazing sites. But they had finally arrived!

In Oregon City, the settlers found stores, newspapers, churches, blacksmith's shops, mills, and other signs of a growing city. It was a relief to finally stop traveling.

But everyone wanted land. That was why they had traveled so far. Families quickly spread out in different directions, hunting for the acres they would soon call home. They had traveled for months on the Oregon Trail, and now they would settle the western United States. The dreams that carried these courageous pioneers across America would now be realized.

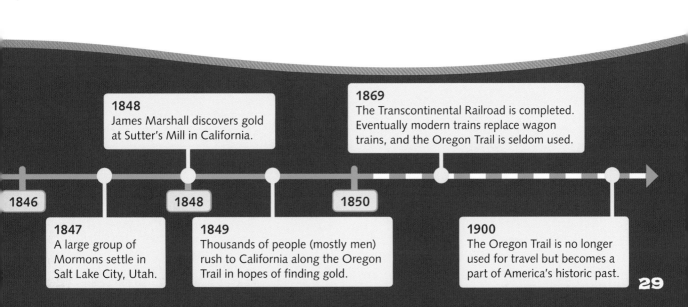

1848
James Marshall discovers gold at Sutter's Mill in California.

1869
The Transcontinental Railroad is completed. Eventually modern trains replace wagon trains, and the Oregon Trail is seldom used.

1846

1848

1850

1847
A large group of Mormons settle in Salt Lake City, Utah.

1849
Thousands of people (mostly men) rush to California along the Oregon Trail in hopes of finding gold.

1900
The Oregon Trail is no longer used for travel but becomes a part of America's historic past.

GLOSSARY

cholera (KAH-luhr-uh)—a dangerous disease that causes severe sickness and diarrhea; cholera is caused by contaminated food or water

Continental Divide (kahn-tuh-NEN-tuhl duh-VYD)—an invisible line that splits North America into two parts

dung (DUHNG)—solid waste from animals

gorge (GORJ)—a canyon with steep walls that rise straight upward

migrate (MYE-grate)—to move from one place to another

portage (POOR-tij)—to carry a boat or supplies over land from one stretch of water to another

provisional government (pruh-VIZH-uh-nuhl GUHV-urn-muhnt)—a temporary government; the provisional government of the Oregon Country served as a temporary form of government until Oregon became a state

READ MORE

Doeden, Matt. *The Oregon Trail: An Interactive History Adventure.* You Choose. North Mankato, Minn.: Capstone Press, 2014.

Figley, Marty Rhodes. *Clara Morgan and the Oregon Trail Journey.* History Speaks: Picture Books Plus Reader's Theater. Minneapolis: Millbrook Press, 2011.

Friedman, Mel. *The Oregon Trail.* Cornerstones of Freedom. New York: Children's Press, 2013.

Marciniak, Kristin. *The Oregon Trail and Westward Expansion.* Perspectives Library. Ann Arbor, Mich.: Cherry Lake Publishing, 2013.

INTERNET SITES

FactHound offers a safe, fun way to find Internet sites related to this book. All of the sites on FactHound have been researched by our staff.

Here's all you do:

Visit *www.facthound.com*

Type in this code: 9781491401873

Check out projects, games and lots more at
www.capstonekids.com

CRITICAL THINKING USING THE COMMON CORE

1. Name three reasons why so many people decided to move out West during the 1800s. (Key Ideas and Details)

2. Look at the diagram of the prairie schooner on page 11. How does the info graphic help you better understand the text on the page and the life of the pioneers in general? (Integration of Knowledge and Ideas)

3. Would you have liked to have been one of the settlers that traveled on the Oregon Trail? Why or why not? (Text Types and Purposes)

INDEX